DUSTY ROADS AUSTRALIA

DUSTY ROADS AUSTRALIA

BOOK OF THE ROAD FOR
OVER SEAS TRAVELERS

Peter Proudlock

Copyright © 2021 by Peter Proudlock

All rights reserved. No part of this book may be reproduced in any form or by any electronic or mechanical means, including information storage and retrieval systems, without permission in writing from the publisher, except by reviewers, who may quote brief passages in a review.

ISBN: 978-1-956736-91-5 (Paperback Edition)
ISBN: 978-1-956736-92-2 (Hardcover Edition)
ISBN: 978-1-956736-90-8 (E-book Edition)

Some characters and events in this book are fictitious. Any similarity to the real persons, living or dead, is coincidental and not intended by the author.

Book Ordering Information

Phone Number: 315 288-7939 ext. 1000 or 347-901-4920
Email: info@globalsummithouse.com
Global Summit House
www.globalsummithouse.com

Printed in the United States of America

Big Red Kangaroos having a nap in Central Australia

Dedication

I dedicate this book to my children Jamie and Jessie Ann, for without their inspiration and tenacity over the years I may have not have been so inspired to continue with my dream.

PETER PROUDLOCK

CONTENTS

Introduction 11
Trip Decision 12
Vehicle Preparation 13
Tyres And Tyre Pressures 15
Spare Parts For My Vehicle 16
Tools 17
What Personal Spares Do I Need For The Trip 18
How To Pack Your Vehicle 19
Pets 20
Towing A Caravan Or Camper Trailer 21
Night Driving 22
Driving On Unsealed Roads 23
Technology 24
New Drivers To Australia 25
Trains, Railway Crossings And Boom Gates 26
Survival 28
Setting Up A Bush Camp 29
Budgeting 31
Epilogue 39

The Authors Rights

Dusty Roads Australia
Book Of The Road

INTRODUCTION

Hello, if you are a new adventurer to Australia or a repeat visitor a very big welcome to you. My name is Peter Proudlock, over the past 30 years I have travelled extensively throughout the outback of Australia both as an Australian Army Soldier and also as a tourist just like yourselves who just wants to get out and see what this wonderful country has to offer which most people have only seen on television or at the movies. In saying that, television and movies showing you all of the wonders and beauty of the country don't always show or explain the hidden dangers as well. In this book I am I will give you some examples of what you may come across when travelling by road around Australia so you will have a safe and journey.

I feel that confidence in yourself and your vehicle has a lot to do with your decision whether or not you undertake a journey to travel any Australian roads, Sealed or Unsealed. In this book I hope to alleviate some of your fears about making such a journey. A lot of like minded people like you had the same fears and worries; I use to be one of them. I had a good teacher in the Australian Defence Force (Army Transport Corps) who taught me not only how to survive in the outback but also how to prepare vehicles correctly for such a trip no matter where you want to go, and by passing on my knowledge I know this book will help you.

TRIP DECISION

It is very exciting watching your favourite outback adventure show on the TV or DVD and how people drive their 4WD around the outback, through river crossings and across sand dunes on the road less travelled and all you can think of is I can't wait to do the same, but what you have to remember is those people have had at least some experience driving on outback roads and they have prepared their vehicles accordingly. Maybe ask a few friends who have done a 4WD trip and get some tips from them. No matter where you decide to go for your very first out back road adventure you need to prepare yourself and your vehicle.

Is your first trip going to be for two or three weeks or just a couple of days? I would suggest you undertake a small trip first say two or three days so you get to know how your vehicle handles in different conditions and whether or not you have packed too much gear or not enough, this will also give you a chance to see how your vehicle set up may handle an extended trip and what requirements the vehicle may need for an more extended drive especially if you and your vehicle are only used to city driving. Before leaving for your trip always let someone know where you are going, give them your trip plan and let them know when you should be back. Keep in contact with them during your trip just to let them know you are ok. As an overseas visitor if you don't know anybody in Australia you can contact the local Police station and advise them of your travel plans. This is a good safety measure.

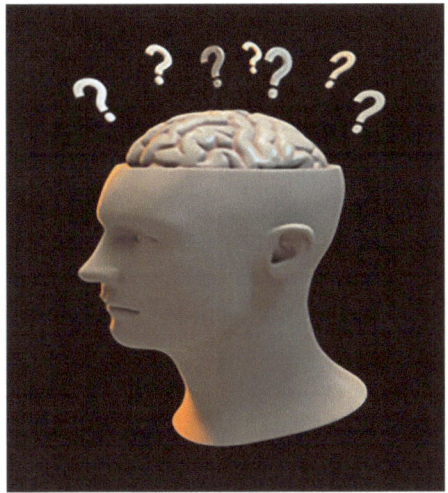

VEHICLE PREPARATION

When you decide which way you are going to be travelling it will be a very important decision on how you outfit your vehicle. (Make sure you have a Road worthy and reliable vehicle). Coming from overseas, if you don't have any friends in Australia who can advise you please do some research on the vehicle you may want to hire. Depending on where you are going, your destination decision will affect what to take on your vehicle. What type of vehicle will you be driving on your journey? It's not preferable to take a small two wheel drive vehicle to say the Bloomfield Track in Far North Queensland. You really need a 4WD Vehicle in my opinion. In saying that most roads in recent years have been sealed, however I know from experience that there are still a lot of unsealed outback roads as well that a small 2WD vehicle with road tyres is just not designed to negotiate and you could find yourself in some bother. Look at the trip you want to undertake and say to yourself; is my vehicle up to the task?

Make sure you have your vehicle fully serviced before you go, and tell the mechanic you are undertaking a big trip and ask him/her if they would conduct a safety inspection of the vehicle to insure its roadworthiness.

This also includes any towed vehicle you may be taking. Make sure if it is a trailer or a caravan that you have the wheel bearings checked to make sure they are serviceable. Towing points and wiring checked as well. Make sure you have 'Rated D Shackles' for attaching safety chains from your towed vehicle to the vehicle you are driving. The police are very strict when it comes to the strength and capacity of towing chains and D Shackles and I know from experience they will pull you over and check. Not to mention the safety aspect as well of properly rated chains and shackles.

TYRES AND TYRE PRESSURES

You will also need a good set of tyres.   I use all terrain tyres on my 4WD.   I also use light truck tyres on my caravan as well.   It pays to do some research on the tyres you may require for your intended adventure.   Ask the staff of your local tyre store, their knowledge will be invaluable.   Use recommended tyre pressures from the manufacturer.

SPARE PARTS FOR MY VEHICLE

- Make yourself a check list for your vehicle (these below are suggested parts only, all vehicles are different).
- Globes front and rear
- Fuses, if you're not sure what type you need speak to your mechanic.
- Windscreen wiper blades
- Fan belt
- Radiator hoses Water/coolant for your radiator
- Engine oil
- Brake fluid
- Fuel jerry cans
- Brake down reflectors
- Tarps
- 2-6 meter chain
- Snatch Strap
- Tree Protector
- Tyre Inflation Gauge

TOOLS

A descent tool set consisting of ring spanners, socket set, screw driver set, electrical wire connection and clamping set, a good set of pliers with side cutters and a hammer.

Good tyre punctures repair kit.

On a long trip you may need to take spare fuel as well. If your vehicle normally gets around 500kms to a tank of fuel, remember you will be carrying extra weight you need to take enough fuel to compensate. Also if you are on dirt roads that are hard going and you need to be in 4wd (which you should be in on dirt roads for better control), you will also use more fuel.

You may think this is a lot but when you are on the road you have to be self sufficient, there isn't going to be a fuel station or a mechanic to get you out of trouble on every corner, because most times in remote areas there isn't any.

Be prepared.

WHAT PERSONAL SPARES DO I NEED FOR THE TRIP

The biggest suggestion I could make is if you are on an extended trip take plenty of spare drinking water and food. Water in the outback is worth more than gold or opals. If you are travelling remote outback roads there isn't always going to be a tap handy to get water from, not like in the city so you need to be self sufficient and carry plenty of water with you. In the extremes of the summer heat in parts of the outback when it is around 47 to 50 degrees you will be thanking you're lucky stars you are carrying plenty of water. My rule of thumb is I carry 20 litres of water for the radiator or spare coolant if needed and 40 litres of drinking water for myself. Don't forget extra water for cooking and washing.

Depending on how long you intend to be away, you don't need lots of clothes. Two or three changes should be sufficient. Take plenty of one and two dollar coins for the laundrettes you may use in some towns or caravan parks, depends where you are staying. You can always wash your clothes by hand if needed. Use a small collapsible tub to wash your clothes in, PLEASE do not wash your clothes in a river, creek or a dam, this water in the outback is the lifeblood of famers and their stock and you will only pollute the water and the stock can't drink it and they will die. Most caravan parks in the outback provide good resources like showers, toilets etc as part of the cost of entry, however some more remote areas have to charge extra for showers and laundry facilities. Some showers have a metered box in the shower cubicle where you put your dollar coins in to receive your shower water which usually last approx 5 mins.

Don't forget to get yourself a comprehensive first aid kit, make sure you know how to use it because your life or somebody else's life may depend on it. I am a qualified first aider and I suggest that someone in your family or group also be qualified in case of a medical emergency on the road.   Don't forget your toiletries, a good strong broad brim hat to keep the sun off, sunscreen, insect repellent, fly net to cover your head, good ankle high boots may protect against a snake strike. Thongs won't stop a sharp stick or a bit of wire going into your foot although thongs are good to wear in the showers at caravan parks.

HOW TO PACK YOUR VEHICLE

When packing your vehicle for your adventure, make sure you pack your non essentials in first.   Nothing worse than travelling happily down the road and you get a flat tyre, you open the boot or the back of your vehicle and you can't find your jack or wheel changing equipment because it's underneath everything else. Also do not over load your vehicle.   I have seen too many times vehicles and trailers sitting on the side of the road with broken axles due to overloading.

PETS

Before leaving on your adventure it is best to ensure your pet immunisations are up to date. If you decide to take your pet, remember that not all Caravan Parks allow pets. Contact the caravan parks that you are going to be staying in along your route and ask if they allow family pets. Some caravan parks may allow, they can ask for their immunisation paperwork as a precaution. Also National Parks throughout the country I found will not allow pets unless prior arrangements have been made. I was surprised, at the amount of Australian tourist destinations I could not visit because they did not allow pets. Also on hot days when you are thirsty, don't forget your family pet will be thirsty as well. When travelling it is best to know the plants and animals to be aware of that may cause harm to your pet in the areas that you are in. Look for signage of dangers and toxins that are being used such as weed killers or feral animal baits, keep animals on a lead for their safety.

TOWING A CARAVAN OR CAMPER TRAILER

If you have never towed a caravan or a camper trailer, talk to someone who owns one and who can give you helpful hints and tips on how to tow. If not go and talk the experts who sell these vehicles, they will help you. Knowledge is invaluable when towing any vehicle. Get some practice on towing and also reversing, this will help you when moving into caravan parks and squeezing between other campers and their rigs.

Is your towing vehicle suitable for towing your caravan or camper trailer? It is illegal and highly dangerous to tow for example an 8 meter dual axle caravan weighing in at around 2.5 to 3 ton with a vehicle which only weighs 1 ton. You cannot possibly expect your one ton vehicle to pull up a 2.5 or 3 ton caravan. Your heavier caravan will just continue to push you forward simply with its weight and momentum especially on downhill mountain roads which will result in a bad outcome. Again talk to the right people about the correct choice of caravan or camper trailer to suit your towing vehicle.

Always remember when towing, your vehicle will behave differently because of the added weight. It will take longer to stop, your steering will react differently also, you have to take all of these points into consideration. Always remember to drive to the road conditions. Keep your windows wound up when moving at speeds over 60 km/hr. If you leave your windows down it creates drag on your vehicle which in turn will make you use more fuel. It will cost you less to use your Air Con.

NIGHT DRIVING

I don't recommend driving at night unless you have to drive to the next safe area to pull up for the night, or in an emergency.

Main reasons being the abundance of wildlife which is out and about at night, Kangaroos, Wallabies, Wombats, Sheep, Cattle, Goats and Wild pigs and the list goes on.   All of which can cause an accident jumping onto the road in front of you at night. Black cattle cannot be seen at night while they are standing still on a road in front of you, unless they blink their eyes which will then reflect in your headlights.   By then it may be too late to stop.   If you have to drive during the night please make sure you have a good set of driving spot lights fitted for seeing at a greater distance on outback and country roads at night and slow down.

Please be courteous to oncoming vehicles by dipping your high beam lights in plenty of time so you don't blind the driver.

At night on an outback or country road I recommend slowing to a speed 10 to 20 kilometres under the legal speed limit. Drive to the weather conditions and the road conditions. I would rather get to my destination later than expected than not at all.

DRIVING ON UNSEALED ROADS

Driving on an unsealed road is a lot more difficult than driving on sealed road. An unsealed surface may include dirt, sand, gravel and water. All of these roads can also have different difficulties depending on road conditions at the time. Rain can make gravel and dirt roads not only slippery and dangerous but sometimes impassable. Be aware of weather conditions, tune in to your local radio station or ask a local and make an informed decision on your travel. Driving on unsealed roads you must decrease your speed and if you are driving on a dusty road with other vehicles in front of you increase the distance between vehicles so you can see the road in front clearly. River or creek crossings are very dangerous, if you can't see the bottom of the crossing and there is a lot of water flow. Do not cross. Find another way to your destination or wait until the water level has dropped to a safe level. Never cross a flooded causeway or river crossing. However once you have crossed the river or creek and are safely on the other side gently apply your brakes to ensure they work. Wet brakes make it harder for a vehicle to stop please be aware of that.

TECHNOLOGY

On my recent adventures across the Nullarbor Plains towing my caravan I decided to stop for a week at Eucla on the Western Australia side of the border between South Australia and Western Australia. I absolutely loved the area, just myself and my dog Zodie who travels everywhere with me. I tried to make a phone call to friends and family to let them know I had arrived safely using my mobile phone. I soon realised I didn't have reception, in fact I didn't have reception for the whole week I was there. Lucky there was a pay phone in the caravan park which I was able to use.

Before travelling the outback, check with your Mobile Phone service provider to see if you can get reception in the areas that you wish to travel, especially in case of an emergency. If you can't get reception as a suggestion you may want to invest in a Satellite Phone which are not cheap or maybe rent one for the duration of your trip which would work out to be cheaper. Also you can invest in a Personal Locator Beacon (PLB) which would be Invaluable in an extreme emergency.

You can buy the PLB online or from most camping and boating stores.

Always carry a paper map with you that way if you do not have reception or you are unable to use GPS you do not get lost. Also you can work out your next day's travel and work out distances between fuel and rest stops.

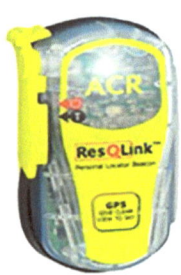

NEW DRIVERS TO AUSTRALIA

First you must drive on the LEFT side of the road. Oncoming traffic will pass you on the Right side (Drivers Side) of your vehicle. Be aware of Australian wildlife, most sealed roads have warning signs of animal crossings in the area so be aware and vigilant at all times.

When refuelling your vehicle be aware that when paying you must do so inside the garage, unlike European and other overseas service stations where you can pay with a credit card at the pump.

In saying that, there are a few self serve fuel stops where you can use your credit card at the pump starting to spring up around the country in more isolated areas.

Australia is a vast area, and on longer more remote driving trips long distances between service stations are not uncommon. Be aware of your fuel and water consumption. Ensure you have a break from driving every 2 hours. Fatigue is a big killer of people on our roads, so when you are tired, please pull over and have a sleep when it is safe to do so.

DANGERS

On our more remote roads the speed limits vary so please be aware of the legal driving limits which are in Kilometres per hour, not Miles per hour. Be very cautious of our wildlife such as Kangaroos, Birds, Wombats, Goats, Sheep just to name a few especially during the hour's of sunset and sunrise.

Big Trucks and (Road Trains, which tow multiple trailers) frequent most roads, please give them the courtesy of moving over in your lane when they pass you coming in the opposite direction. When overtaking a Road Train or any larger vehicle remember, that you have to give them more room because of the extra length and width of their vehicle. If you are driving a 2wd vehicle on an unsealed (dirt) road please slow down to a speed where you can stop quickly if you need to. While travelling on these roads they can be very hazardous. Passing another a vehicle on a dirt road please pass slowly as to not flick dirt and rocks up from your tyres, which may impact on their vehicles windscreen.

TRAINS, RAILWAY CROSSINGS AND BOOM GATES

Australia has a vast network of railway lines which criss-crosses the country with a total 36,064 kilometres (22, 409 miles) of track as at 2018 on three major track gauges. Monster heavy trains can be found hauling everything from passengers, coal, iron ore, salt, and general cargo just to name a few. The total length of one freight train was an impressive 5.5 kilometers (3.4 miles) in length.

Iron ore trains in Australia consist of up to 236 wagons, each having a load capacity of up to 106 tonnes. These trains are up to 2.4 kilometers (1.5 miles) in length and fully loaded can weigh approximately 29,500 tonnes.

These statistics above gives you an Idea of the size and weight of some of the trains you may come across when traversing the country.

This is why when you are driving whether it is in the cities or on country roads that you always be on the lookout for trains when approaching a level crossing with or without Boom Gates, Stop signs or Warning Lights. Just because there are electronic warning devices on most crossings it doesn't mean they all work, especially on outback or country roads.

If you are approaching a rail crossing slow down to a speed where you can stop if necessary, look both ways and only cross when it is safe to do so. Most country rail crossings have at least stop signs so please for your safety and the safety of others obey all warnings signs and be aware of your surroundings. It is easier for your one to 3 ton vehicle to stop and give way to an oncoming train than it is for a train weighing 29,000 tonnes to stop for you.

SURVIVAL

Let's say you decided to take your adventure one step further and drive down the road less travelled and get lost or your vehicle breaks down. You have no phone reception, and there is no other vehicles insight because you are so far off the beaten track. The first thing to do is DON'T PANIC. If needed, find a shady spot under a tree near your vehicle to sit, or if there isn't any trees you should carry a tarp in your vehicle that you can use as a shelter from the sun. Stay with or near your vehicle; do not walk off into the open country. If you have been missing for a while a search party will come looking for you. Your vehicle is much easier to find in the outback than a single person. More than likely a farmer or cattle station owner will come by and stop. It's an unspoken law in remote bushland and the outback to stop if you see a vehicle that's on the side of the road and ask if they require help.

If you need to you can attract attention by possibly using your rear view mirrors from your vehicle to reflect light or start a smoky fire using green shrubs that should attract farmers and/or station owners. The last thing they want to see is a fire on their property so they will come to investigate. If you don't have green shrub to burn to make smoke, you can burn the tires on your vehicle which will make black smoke and is a distress signal recognised by most country folk. Carrying sterilisation tablets are a good idea to sterilise brackish drinking water you may find in a dam or stream. Also a ground signal using whatever is available, branches or rocks etc, you can use is SOS or an X which means that you are in trouble and need help. Both should be placed on the ground large enough in size so it can be seen from a passing plane. Thanks to modern technology, in an extreme emergency you can activate your Personal Location Beacon.

Remember, DON'T PANIC and stay with your vehicle and you will be ok.

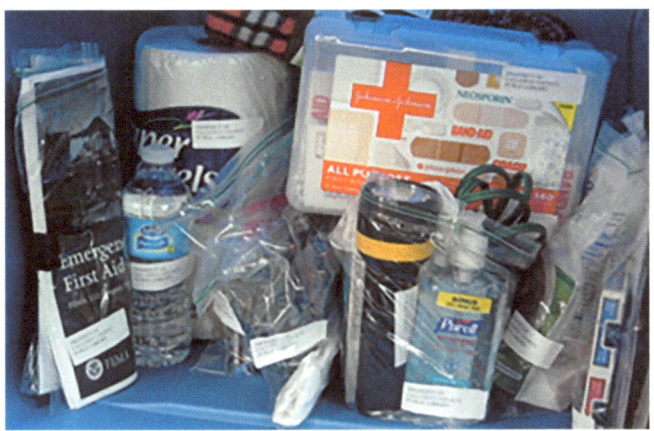

SETTING UP A BUSH CAMP

- When setting up a bush camp, always clear an area from leaves, rocks, branches and debris
- When having an open fire make sure the area is clear from anything that may alight drastically
- Set up a bucket of water next to the fire
- Keep any food off the ground
- Moving around your new camp vigorously and creating noise will keep most snakes away as well. They are more scared of you than you are of them.
- Once you have settled in to camp, check the underneath of your vehicle for any oil leaks and any damages.
- Before departing your campsite lift your bonnet and check oil and water levels before starting the engine

PREPARING FOR BED

- Before going to bed once you have removed your shoes ensure any openings are covered so they are protected from creepy crawlies, always zip up your tent before going to sleep.
- If you are in the bush for an extended amount of time when you wake up check your boots, tip them upside down so if there is anything inside it falls out, during the day while you are not at your camp roll your sleeping bag back up so nothing can get inside, always check for anything inside, zip up tent whenever exiting.
- Remove any rubbish from the campsite, take it with you.
- If anyone in the family smokes please check they are disposing of them into a ashtray or into a fire so they are not left on the ground
- Check the area you are camping in if they are in a fire ban and if so DONT have a fire.
- Before leaving any camping spot always make sure that your campfire is completely out.

BUDGETING

- It is important to budget correctly for when going on a long trip as you may end up with unpredictable expenses such as car maintenance, and extra fuel.
- Ensure you have a decent amount of cash for small purchases to a avoid Eftpos fees.
- Switch Low Fee cards so you can avoid any extra ATM fees.
- Plan and book ahead for your caravan parks or cheap motels, you may find that the closer to the trip you book it may be harder to get a spot depending on time of year.
- When booking ahead and planning your trip take into a count the time of year and the popularity of your destination, I recommend travelling to the below destinations between end of April to end of October;
- Northern Territory, Northern NSW, QLD and Western Australia.
- Charging devices – need a pure sine inverter, recommend using a 300 WATT for average charging needs.
- Generator size will depend on devices you want to charge or generate power for. 2-2.5 KVA generator for families will run camp fridge, TV, lights – depending on amount of devices, you may be able to use a smaller size generator to run less devices.
- Bug Zappers
- Lights – torches
- A suited to climate sleeping bag

ROAD MAPS

The following are maps of Australian states and I have detailed some of the roads I have travelled to hopefully get your travel juices flowing. I thoroughly recommend these trips or you can make your own adventures. So if you are off on a weekend drive or you are looking to travel a greater distance dont let the dust settle behind you, get on the road, Australia is calling.

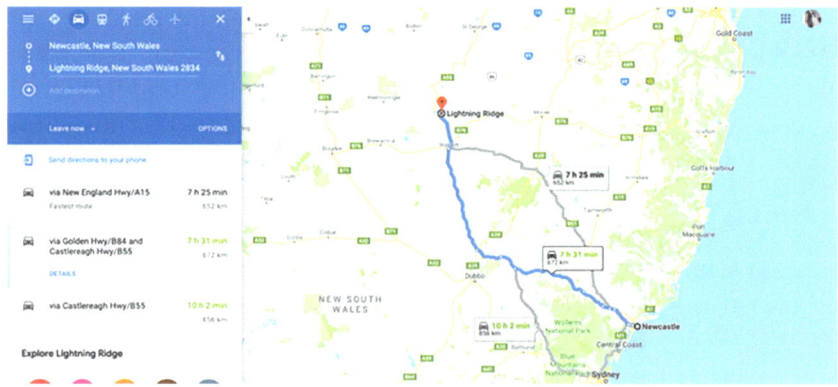

Newcastle to Lightning Ridge NSW showing alternative routes

Newcastle NSW to Cook town Far North Queensland via east coast

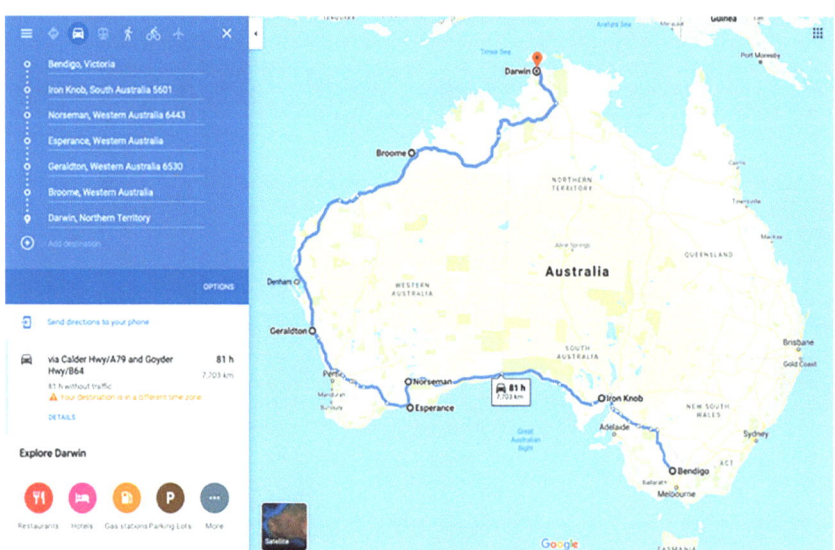

Bendigo Victoria to Darwin in the Northern Territory via Western Australia

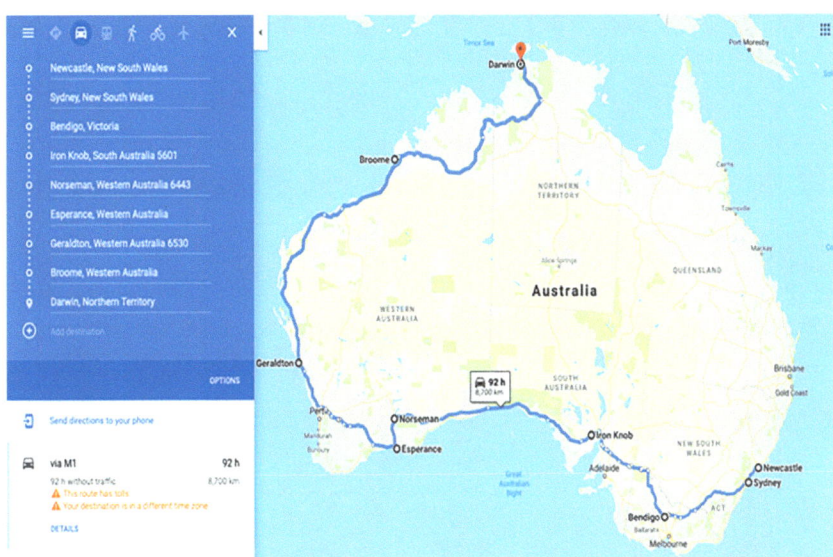

Newcastle NSW to Darwin in the Northern Territory via Bendigo Victoria and Western Australia

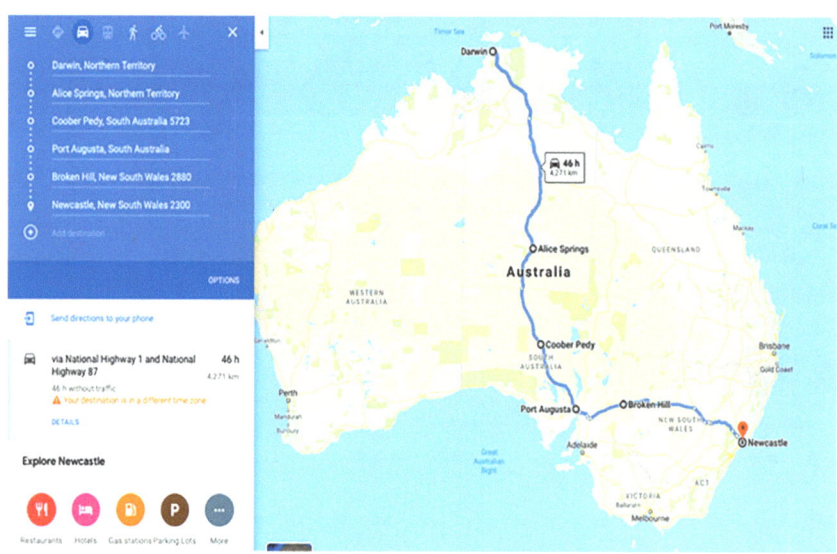

Newcastle NSW to Darwin in the Northern Territory via South Australia.

Camel Riding Stuarts Well Central Australia

Peter Proudlock

EPILOGUE

I wish you and your loved ones many happy journeys through and around this great country and always remember that not every journey is smooth and trouble free. Be prepared and remember the 5 P's I learnt in the Military. Prior Preparation Prevents Poor Performance.

See you on the road.

Your Author Peter (Proudy) Proudlock

www.ingramcontent.com/pod-product-compliance
Lightning Source LLC
LaVergne TN
LVHW070436080526
838202LV00034B/2653